# LAINEY WILSON

# The Heartbeat of Country Music

MATTIE SNOW

## Copyright @ 2024 By Mattie Snow

All rights reserved. No part of this book may be reproduced, distributed, or transmitted in any form or by any means, including photocopying, recording, or other electronic or mechanical methods, without the prior written permission of the publisher, except in the case of brief quotations embodied in critical reviews and specific other noncommercial uses permitted by copyright law.

# Contents

**INTRODUCTION**
    The Heartbeat Begins
**CHAPTER 1: ROOTS IN A SMALL TOWN**
    Growing Up in Baskin, Louisiana
    Early Musical Influences
**CHAPTER 2: THE ROAD TO NASHVILLE**
    Moving to Music City
    Challenges and Breakthroughs
**CHAPTER 3: CRAFTING HER SOUND**
    Writing Her Own Songs
    Blending Country with Personal Storytelling
**CHAPTER 4: RISING STAR**
    The Release of Her First Album
    Gaining Recognition in the Industry
**CHAPTER 5: THE BREAKTHROUGH MOMENT**
    Hit Singles and Chart Success
    Collaborations with Other Artists
**CHAPTER 6: THE HEART OF THE FANS**
    Building a Dedicated Fanbase
    Engaging with Her Audience

**CHAPTER 7: LIFE ON THE ROAD**
    Touring Experiences
    Balancing Fame and Personal Life

**CHAPTER 8: ADVOCACY AND IMPACT**
    Using Her Platform for Change
    Community Involvement and Philanthropy

**CHAPTER 9: PERSONAL STRUGGLES AND TRIUMPHS**
    Navigating Challenges Behind the Scenes
    Overcoming Obstacles in Her Career

**CHAPTER 10: THE FUTURE OF COUNTRY MUSIC**
    Lainey's Vision for the Genre
    Mentoring the Next Generation of Artists

**CONCLUSION**
    Reflections on Her Journey

# INTRODUCTION

## The Heartbeat Begins

Lainey Wilson discovered her groove in the heart of Louisiana, where the sounds of country music permeate the land and pierce the spirits of those who live there. She was reared in the rich tradition of southern storytelling and the poignant ballads that could be heard everywhere, having been born in the tiny town of Baskin. Her early years were shaped by the expansive fields, the rolling hills, and the resounding laughter of her close-knit community. These elements helped to shape her goals and dreams. She dreamed at an early age of becoming more than just a singer; she wanted to develop into a voice that could speak to anybody who dared to dream, expressing the joys, challenges, and victories of daily life.

Eventually, Lainey's path would bring her to Nashville, a city known for its dazzling lights and the promise of stardom. Nonetheless, the core of her music will always beat to the rhythm of her upbringing in the South, giving each note a rich tapestry of experiences. She stays firmly rooted in the principles that her parents instilled in her throughout her early years—a strong commitment to authenticity, connection, and storytelling—even while she negotiates the complexity of the music industry.

Lainey Wilson is a force that personifies the essence of contemporary country music, not just a name in the credits. Her music embodies the essence of vulnerability, love, and resiliency with a distinctive blend of classic sounds and modern flair. Her songs are a reflection of her experiences in life, each one vividly rendered with lyrics that speak to listeners well beyond the confines of her city. She invites listeners to join her on her journey and see parallels between their own lives in her songs as she infuses personal tales into her melodies, bringing them into her universe.

"Lainey Wilson: The Heartbeat of Country Music," a biography, explores the life of an extraordinary musician who is redefining what it means to be a modern-day country star. We examine the critical events that molded Lainey into the artist she is today, from her upbringing in a close-knit town to her ascent to the top of the charts. Along the process, readers will experience the ups and downs of chasing a dream, the sacrifices made, and the tremendous influence of her music on a generation of people looking for inspiration and connection.

Lainey's tale is one of perseverance and grace, in which each obstacle is used as a springboard for achievement. It includes the innumerable evenings devoted to penning songs that would ultimately turn into vulnerable and empowering anthems—songs that resonate with listeners and encourage them to accept who they really are. It encapsulates the thrill of performing live when she engages with crowds that draw strength and comfort from her words, fostering moments of exuberance and catharsis.

This voyage has its challenges, though. In a career that may sometimes feel isolated, the weight of expectations, periods of uncertainty, and the unwavering desire for self-acceptance are hidden behind the limelight. Lainey's resoluteness to remain loyal to herself in the face of social pressure to fit in is indicative of her genuineness as a person and an artist. It is evidence of the difficulties people encounter when pursuing their passions, and Lainey's tenacity offers encouragement to others who choose to walk in her shoes.

We will get to know the friends, family, and mentors who have shaped Lainey's journey as we flip the pages of this book. We will learn the backstories of her songs, including how her tears and laughter have inspired her, how her happy and sad times have fueled her creativity, and how her stubborn independence has defined her artistic style. Every chapter will showcase not just the musician Lainey has developed into but also the person who lives behind the songs—someone who aspires to establish a strong bond with her listeners and reassure them that they are never alone in their experiences.

In addition to being a gifted musician, Lainey Wilson inspires hope in the hearts of budding artists everywhere with every note she sings and every tale she tells. Lainey breaks free from the limitations of a society that frequently tries to identify and classify artists, establishing an environment where genuineness is valued above all else. Her journey is a celebration of the ability of music to bring people together, heal, and inspire; it inspires us all to discover our voice and tell our experiences to the world. Lainey Wilson is at the front of the country music movement, poised to pave the way for a time when all tales have a place in the spotlight.

# CHAPTER 1: ROOTS IN A SMALL TOWN

## Growing Up in Baskin, Louisiana

The town of Baskin, which is tucked away in the center of Louisiana, has a cadence of existence that is as leisurely and calming as the swaying cypress trees that line its streets. It has a population of just over a thousand people, perfectly capturing the allure of small-town America. Lainey Wilson's journey started here, in the place where the perfume of magnolia fills the air and crickets sing in the evenings. This modest environment served as more than simply the background to her early years; it was also the ideal environment for her ambitions to blossom.

Lainey was raised surrounded by the rich cultural fabric of the South. Being brought up in a family that valued music, she was exposed to her heritage's sounds from a young age. Her father loved country music and would play songs by icons like Willie Nelson and Dolly Parton throughout their house. Each lyric created vivid images of love, grief, and hope, and the flickering radio in the kitchen was a constant reminder of the narrative power of music. This wasn't just background noise for little Lainey; rather, it was an awakening that spurred a desire that would later support her artistic endeavors.

The tight-knit group at Baskin was advantageous as well as difficult. Lainey was frequently the focus of attention because everyone knew each other's business and not simply because of her talents but also because of her dreams, which seemed bigger than the town. She experienced the contradiction of small-town life as a lively child with an obvious spark: the comfort of familiarity as opposed to the desire for something more. Lainey's mind sparkled with pictures of vast stages and audiences swooning to her singing while her pals played in the sun-drenched fields.

Lainey's environment had a big impact on her as she went through her early years. Her awareness of the complexity of life was shaped by the stories told by the community's elders, the customs that have been passed down through the centuries, and the tender get-togethers around bonfires following a demanding workday. She incorporated these experiences into her songwriting, learning to find beauty in both the every day and the spectacular. Every smile fueled her imagination, giggle, and tears she shed.

Days at school were filled with that same mixture of anticipation and anxiety that many children feel. Lainey was a budding performer in addition to a student. Her skill was evident to everyone around her, whether she was singing in the school talent show or taking part in church choir performances. Both professors and students started to laud her voice for its richness and soulfulness. But pressure also followed recognition. Lainey was burdened by expectations from the community that had raised her as well as from herself. Would she follow their ambitions for herself, or would she forge her course?

Lainey frequently turned to nature for comfort during her quiet times. The expansive vistas of Louisiana served as more than just a backdrop; they served as a wellspring of creativity. As she strolled through the verdant bayous, she was astounded by the complex dance of sunshine penetrating the trees and creating whimsical shadows on the ground. Her songs' rich imagery would eventually be derived from these quiet times of introspection. Her feelings were entwined with the natural beauty of her surroundings, providing her with a distinct viewpoint that would distinguish her as an artist.

Her family greatly influenced Lainey's upbringing. Her identity was shaped by the qualities her parents instilled in her, including tenacity and genuineness. Relatives would often share songs and anecdotes that tied them to their heritage during family get-togethers. These instances strengthened the sense of belonging and community and confirmed the notion that music was a shared experience rather than merely a solo endeavor. Lainey discovered that every note had a story to tell and that music could unite people and spark a passion that would follow her into the future.

But like any young idealist, Lainey had her share of insecurities. It was evident that aspiration and reality were at odds. As she grew older, doubts started to surface regarding her goal and whether a career in music would be feasible. Nevertheless, she found strength in her beliefs despite the uncertainty. Her community's stories of tenacity gave her the willpower to endure, igniting her resolve to escape the constraints of small-town expectations and pursue her goals with unyielding persistence.

She developed her craft over the years, penning her songs and delving further into her imagination. Each song reflected her experiences, fusing her goals with the influences of her background. She mastered the craft of storytelling at Baskin, and she put everything into songs that captured the spirit of her life with each note she sang.

Lainey Wilson's upbringing in Baskin, Louisiana, set the groundwork for her destiny. It was a place that encouraged her goals and pushed her to overcome obstacles. Her music is centered around the lessons she learned, the songs she sang, and the love she shared in this little community. Lainey brought the essence of Baskin with her when she entered the bigger stage of life. This energy would strike a chord with viewers throughout the nation and serve as a constant reminder of the foundation that molded her path and the passion that drives her creative endeavors.

## Early Musical Influences

Long before Lainey Wilson ever stepped onto a stage, her musical adventure started. It was ingrained in her early years, a diverse tapestry of sounds and tales that molded her personality and sparked her love of music and vocal performance. Lainey's upbringing in Baskin,

Louisiana, exposed her to a wide range of musical influences that would greatly affect her artistic direction.

Her family was the primary source of her early musical influences. Lainey would often remember warm afternoons in the living room when her father would play country music on his guitar and fill the room with reassuring sounds. Among the many renowned musicians on his playlist were Johnny Cash, Loretta Lynn, and Willie Nelson, to mention a few. With lyrics that evoked strong feelings and vividly depicted situations of life, love, and sorrow, each song served as a lesson in storytelling. Lainey would sit with her eyes wide open, mesmerized by the melodies and the ability of words to arouse emotions and memories. These were crucial times that gave her the drive to discover her voice and the stories she wanted to share.

As a child, Lainey was always captivated by country music's storytelling quality, as each song seemed to be a chapter from a life well lived. She could relate to the lyrics because they reflected her own family's and community's experiences. Thanks to the stories told by her musical heroes, she could see her own world through a lens. They showed her that music could be more than just amusement; it could be a tool for communication and an expression of the indescribable.

Lainey's mother exposed her to a wide range of musical genres, which broadened her taste in music beyond the typical country sounds that filled her home. Lainey was exposed to a wide range of musical genres, from the forceful anthems of rock to the heartfelt harmonies of R&B, which enhanced her comprehension of rhythm and melody. She developed a feeling of variety from the dynamic interplay of several genres, which allowed her to recognize the subtleties of various musical expressions. Later on, she would be able to explore her sound by fusing pop and rock elements with country influences, thanks to this varied base.

Her artistic development was significantly influenced by the local music scene as well. Despite its modest size, Baskin was packed with artists who frequently got together for unofficial jam sessions. Aspiring musicians performed covers of well-known songs and presented their unique compositions at these creative melting pot gatherings. Lainey frequently attended, taking in the enthusiasm and motivation from witnessing her friends perform. She felt a spark lit by the thrill of live music and started dreaming of performing herself. Lainey was inspired to find her voice among the collective creativity of the local musicians and developed a sense of kinship among them as a result of her exposure to grassroots music.

Lainey's first exposure to early musical influences was shaped by her attendance at a concert by one of her favorite country musicians. She was surrounded by a sea of ecstatic fans and sensed an electrifying bond with the music that filled the hall. Lainey came to understand the tremendous effect that a live performance could have—not only on the audience but also on the performer. She was astounded by the singer's command of the stage, telling tales that made some people laugh and cry. This event further cemented her ambition to pursue a career in music, as she saw herself taking the spotlight and telling the world her own story.

She was also inspired by the music of female musicians who were shattering stereotypes in a field that men had historically controlled. For her, celebrities like Faith Hill and Shania Twain served as rays of empowerment. Lainey learned that she could be a force in the music industry and still communicate her emotions honestly from their ability to combine strength and vulnerability. She found that their songs' themes of independence and resiliency struck a deep chord with her, and she used these themes to inspire and encourage people in her music.

Lainey experimented with melodies and lyrics that represented her distinct viewpoint while drawing inspiration from her wide range of inspirations as she started to write her songs. Her songs were built upon the stories of her life in Baskin, combined with the teachings she had learned from her musical idols. She began writing songs that encapsulated the core of her experiences: tales of heartache, love, and the beauty of ordinary moments. As she wrote more, she came to find her voice—a voice that was both uniquely her own and deeply entrenched in her childhood.

# CHAPTER 2: THE ROAD TO NASHVILLE

## Moving to Music City

Lainey Wilson's aspirations were as big as the sky in Louisiana, and her heart started to long for more than her little town had to offer. Her thoughts were filled with the allure of Nashville, also referred to as "Music City," which beckoned her with the prospect of opportunities and fulfilling her dreams. Although it was a risk, Lainey saw it as an essential step toward her goal of becoming a country music performer.

She took the risk of leaving Baskin behind when she was just eighteen years old. Emotions ran high during the bittersweet farewells to friends and family. She was eager to see what was ahead but also very conscious of the consequences of her decision. She had to leave behind her familiar faces, her cozy house, and the safety of her close-knit neighborhood when she moved to Nashville. Still, the city's allure—the center of country music—was too strong to refuse. She embarked on her new life, holding a guitar in one hand and optimism in the other.

Getting to Nashville was an incredible experience. With its vibrant lights, busy streets, and the distinct sound of music filling the air, the city was teeming with life. As Lainey entered a world where aspirations were fervently pursued, she experienced a wave of inspiration. She soon understood, though, that there might be difficulties along the way. Nashville was a city full of aspirational artists, where there was a lot of talent and intense rivalry.

After moving into a small flat, Lainey had to get used to her new situation. She was surrounded by other musicians, each with their own goals and stories to tell; some were seasoned performers, and some were as inexperienced as she was. The city was vibrant, with opportunities for new relationships and partnerships appearing around every corner. However, the immediate thrill was replaced with the sobering knowledge of what it took to pursue a career in music. The music industry's glitzy exterior frequently hides the long hours, relentless work, and perseverance needed to succeed.

Lainey balanced her music career with a variety of odd jobs, such as waiting tables and retail work, to support herself. Although the hustling was tiresome, every shift moved her one step closer to her objective. She worked as a server during the day and devoted her evenings to writing songs and doing open mic nights. Every moment she had to perform in front of an audience was an opportunity to hone her craft and show off her talent. She felt herself becoming more assured of her skills with each note sung and each line spoken.

Lainey learned early on in Nashville how important it is to have a supportive network of fellow artists. She started making connections with musicians who were as passionate about presenting stories via song as she was. They got together at neighborhood honky-tonks, where the air was filled with the sound of guitars and laughter and where up-and-coming performers could take the stage, even for a short while. She was reminded that she wasn't alone in her challenges by the network of support that the sense of camaraderie provided. These encounters further stimulated her creativity, and they exchanged thoughts and perceptions while supporting one another and providing helpful criticism.

Nashville's rich history and music together constituted its essence. Lainey immersed herself in the past experiences of other artists, taking inspiration from their travels. For her, the iconic locations along Broadway, such as the Ryman Auditorium and the Bluebird Café, where innumerable dreams had begun, became sacred ground. Every visit gave her a sense of direction and served as a reminder of the legacy she wanted to leave behind. She frequently saw herself performing on those same stages, singing to a sea of admirers who would find her music relatable. It was a bittersweet mixture of amazement and aspiration.

Lainey began to create her sound as she refined her technique; it was a fusion of Nashville's current components with the classic country influences of her childhood. This combination became her trademark, differentiating her from the plethora of other aspirants vying for recognition in the field. She was a prolific writer who infused her songs with her experiences and feelings, creating narratives that were both realistic and intimate.

But there were obstacles along the way. Rejections started to appear often, and Lainey had periods of uncertainty that caused her to second-guess her choice to pursue music. Sometimes, after a very hard performance or a bad audition, she felt defeated when she got home. However, she discovered that she could find strength in her passion through each setback. These difficult times served as stepping stones, encouraging her to hone her artistic abilities and write from a genuine place.

With unwavering resolve and perseverance, Lainey started to establish a name for herself in the Nashville music industry. Local composers and producers began to take notice of her as they saw her potential and talent. Small-scale opportunities started to present themselves, such as opening for more well-known acts, getting asked to collaborate on songs, and performing at songwriter rounds. Every accomplishment, no matter how minor, increased her self-assurance and strengthened her will to keep moving forward.

Her confidence as an artist grew along with her presence in Nashville. She was becoming a force to be reckoned with in Music City, no longer just a dream-chasing girl from Baskin. With each note she composed and sang, she was getting closer to realizing the aspirations that had seemed so far away.

Lainey Wilson underwent a significant life shift upon moving to Music City, going from an optimistic dreamer to a budding artist. This voyage would create the foundation for a prosperous future for country music, one that was characterized by development, sacrifice, and unrelenting commitment. Lainey forged a route that would eventually take her to the center of the music industry as she rose to the challenges of her new surroundings and found the strength of her spirit in addition to the power of her voice.

## Challenges and Breakthroughs

In the music business, hurdles are a common part of the path to success, and Lainey Wilson's path was no different. She soon learned that chasing her aspirations would come with difficulties as she adapted to her new life in Nashville, but every setback strengthened her will to succeed and persevere.

Lainey's battle to define herself as an artist was one of the biggest obstacles she had to overcome. It was difficult to stand out from the crowd of wannabe musicians in a city full of talented people. Lainey struggled with self-doubt and frequently wondered if her music would be accepted in a market crowded with both well-known musicians and up-and-coming talent. She felt a lot of pressure to live up to industry norms, which made her try out many sounds and looks in an effort to find her voice. She felt, though, that she was losing herself in the process the more she attempted to fit into a template.

One major concern during her early years in Nashville was money. Like a lot of artists, Lainey had to work multiple jobs to support herself. She would work night shifts at stores and restaurants and spend her evenings composing and performing. She could feel herself getting tired, and some nights, the never-ending grind was too much for her. Her creative endeavors were frequently overshadowed by her ongoing concern about paying her bills, which made it difficult for her to concentrate only on her music. However, despite these difficulties, Lainey gained invaluable knowledge about tenacity and time management—skills that will come in handy later on.

A crucial component of the music industry, networking came with its own set of difficulties. Lainey had to develop the confidence necessary to make contacts in Nashville gradually. At first, she was afraid to go to business events and open mic nights because she was afraid she wouldn't be accepted. She knew very well that in a competitive setting, first impressions mattered. Lainey gradually forced herself to step outside of her comfort zone as she came to see that vulnerability was a strength rather than a weakness. She started to develop deep connections with other musicians, songwriters, and producers who saw her potential as each interaction became a building block.

Notwithstanding the difficulties, breakthroughs started to appear frequently when Lainey least anticipated them. One such moment occurred when she impulsively entered a songwriting competition. Following weeks of creating and polishing her talent, Lainey submitted her song to the contest, which offered a venue for up-and-coming artists to exhibit their work. Her efforts were not only confirmed by this recognition, but it also led to additional chances and connections with eager-to-collaborate industry colleagues. She was encouraged to keep going forward by the event, which confirmed her belief that her music could connect with people.

Another crucial event in Lainey's career was her performance at a neighborhood bar that had grown to be a mainstay for emerging performers. After a certain event, a well-known music producer saw her sincerity and stage appearance and approached her. He showed interest in collaborating with her, which felt like a huge step forward for Lainey. It served as a reminder that persistence is worthwhile, and her efforts had not gone unappreciated. This relationship would result in joint endeavors that profoundly influenced her sound and made her more widely known.

Lainey encountered personal obstacles that tried her resolve while she persevered in navigating the industry's intricacies. She felt a lot of pressure to achieve, which occasionally caused worry and self-doubt. She occasionally wondered if she was making the proper decisions to follow her aspirations and felt alone in her challenges. However, Lainey gained insight into the value of mental health and self-care as a result of these difficulties. Her vulnerability gave her strength, and she turned to friends and mentors for assistance. Speaking up about her emotions gave her a sense of empowerment and helped her overcome the loneliness that frequently results with pursuing big dreams.

Her persistent effort started to pay off as the years went by. Success after success brought her one step closer to realizing her goals. Her songs began to become popular, and she was invited to play at prestigious festivals and gatherings. She experienced a rising sense of validation after each performance as she knew that her music touched others. She stands out for her distinctive fusion of modern and traditional rural inspirations, which has helped her carve out a space for herself in the business.

Lainey Wilson grew tougher and stronger as she overcame each obstacle. Her experience with the highs and lows of the music industry molded her character as much as her artistic abilities. Her obstacles—ranging from financial strain to self-doubt—became stepping stones that eventually helped her succeed. Once-unattainable breakthroughs started to appear, Lainey realized that every obstacle was really a prelude to an opportunity for success.

# CHAPTER 3: CRAFTING HER SOUND

## Writing Her Own Songs

The trajectory of Lainey Wilson's career as a composer encapsulates her creative spirit. Writing songs is a lifeline for her, a means of expressing her experience, processing her feelings, and establishing a connection with the outside world. Lainey understood at a young age that the words she wrote had power, and that power increased with the depth of her experiences. Composing her songs turned into a defining feature of her identity as an artist, influencing her career in country music and enabling her to create an unquestionably honest and intimate body of work.

For Lainey, penning songs was second nature. Growing up in the little Louisianan town of Baskin, where people shared stories on porches and around dinner tables, she discovered that music was a tool for communication as well as for listening. She found an intuitive way to translate her ideas and emotions into lyrics when she took up a guitar and began writing songs. Writing songs gave Lainey a voice in a world where she occasionally felt like an alien; it was instinctive, like breathing.

Lainey's choice to write her own songs instead of relying on cover songs initially distinguished her. She felt that being real was more important than having creative control. She felt that she was the best person to convey her experience. By penning her own lyrics, Lainey could bring her own experiences and realities to her songs. Every line and melody reflected her journey's highs and lows, from sadness to hope.

However, penning her music took a lot of work. It demanded openness, a readiness to show the sides of herself that others would be afraid to show. On certain days, Lainey would spend hours sitting in front of her guitar, attempting to put her feelings into words. She was forced to delve deeply and frequently face emotions she wasn't even aware existed. It was a rigorous but therapeutic procedure that had her relieve painful, joyful, and uncertain experiences. But every song that emerged from those sessions served as a tribute to her will to stay true to herself, even in the face of pain.

Lainey had to develop the ability to craft a narrative that was not only relevant but also personal because she was dedicated to writing her music. When people heard her music, she wanted them to feel something. Lainey believed that a great song was about inspiring emotion rather than merely smart lyrics or good hooks. Lainey's songs honestly depicted the human experience, whether it was the warmth of falling in love, the agony of loss, or the nostalgia of remembering where you came from. Every song started to represent both her and her listeners in a mirror image.

A remarkable quality of Lainey's music is her ability to convey intensely personal yet widely relatable experiences. Although she sings about universal topics such as love, heartbreak, perseverance, and growth, she writes about what she knows. Her lyrics reflect her genuineness, and it is this openness that has won her the admiration of both critics and fans. Her talent for fusing reflection with narrative is evident in songs like "Things a Man Oughta Know," which craft an intimate yet relatable story for everyone who has ever dealt with the difficulties of life.

Lainey took influence from her surroundings as well. Many of her compositions were inspired by her regular moments of loneliness, late-night phone calls with friends, and conversations with relatives. Her ability to see the slightest nuances of life and turn them into vibrant, poetic images was remarkable. A peaceful evening at home may inspire a ballad about desire and love, while a straightforward drive down a country road may inspire a song about independence. Lainey saw inspiration all around her, and it was her responsibility to accurately and truthfully convey it.

Lainey developed her songwriting abilities and learned to follow her gut. She came to see that her best songs came from the moments she let go of her overanalyzing and opened herself up to feeling the music. In short spurts of inspiration, she wrote some of her most impactful songs in a matter of minutes, letting the words come to her naturally and without hesitation. She labored over other songs for weeks or months, making sure the words perfectly conveyed the depth of her feelings. Whatever the schedule, Lainey gave every song her all because she knew it would be a reflection of her heart.

Another important aspect of Lainey's songwriting approach was collaboration. She loved writing alone, but she also recognized the beauty that might occur when she collaborated with other songwriters. Nashville became a hub for artistic collaborations, as Lainey would get together with other musicians to exchange concepts, frequently culminating in compositions that merged disparate viewpoints. Through these partnerships, she was able to expand her lyrical horizons and explore a wider spectrum of feelings and narratives, thereby improving her songwriting.

Understanding that flaws were a necessary component of the writing process was one of Lainey's greatest turning points in her songwriting career. She realized that not every song has to be polished or immediately suitable for the radio. Rough versions of several of her best-loved songs were voice memos or notebooks filled with crude lyrics and basic melodies. She would come back to these concepts over time, developing them into something greater but always keeping sight of the original inspiration. Lainey was able to write songs that sounded genuine rather than contrived because she was ready to accept the flaws in them.

Lainey has been able to steer her story in an industry that frequently tries to define musicians according to its standards by penning her songs. She was not going to be simply another country music performer of someone else's songwriting. She wanted to communicate her own story in her voice, and she has succeeded in doing so by writing songs. Every song offers a peek at the woman behind the music and a window into her soul.

# Blending Country with Personal Storytelling

Beyond just a catchy tune, Lainey Wilson's music is an expression of her identity, firmly anchored in the sober, intimate tales that shape her life as well as the classic aspects of country music. Lainey realized early on in her path that country music was about more than just singing appealing songs. It was all about telling stories—tales that stir up feelings, encapsulate the highs and lows of life, and establish a very intimate connection with the audience.

Authenticity has always captivated Lainey as a songwriter. The approach to the craft has been influenced by her idea that the greatest songs originate from a place of truth. Lainey was raised in a community that respected integrity and hard work, and her upbringing in Baskin, Louisiana, served as the basis for the stories she would later sing. Her songs are filled with a depth that relates to universal human experiences. Yet, they also frequently capture the simplicity and beauty of small-town life—family, faith, love, and heartbreak.

Lainey's ability to fuse the genre's conventional storytelling technique with her distinct voice is what makes her stand out in the country music market. Although personal narratives have long been a part of country music, Lainey's songwriting offers an unabashedly real and contemporary viewpoint. Whether it's the difficulties of making ends meet, the intricacies of relationships, or the obstacles of pursuing aspirations in a field that is frequently cruel, she doesn't back down from talking about tough subjects. Her songs are always authentic to her experience, even though they can be vulnerable at times.

She learned as a child to construct a very personal story about self-reliance and resilience in this song. The song has a classic yet modern vibe to it thanks to the way Lainey's modern narrative technique combines with traditional country instruments. Those who related to the song's theme of strength and independence were moved by its insightful reflections about life and love in the lyrics. It's the ideal illustration of how Lainey transforms country music into a dialogue and an emotional interaction between herself and her listeners by using personal narrative.

For Lainey, telling a story is about more than just writing great choruses and hooks. Making her audience feel seen is her goal. Every song is akin to a chapter in her life narrative, although it reflects the experiences of a great many people. She is able to capture the essence of what it is to be human in her music, capturing everything from the ecstasy of love to the anguish of loss and all in between. Lainey's honesty strikes a chord with her fans, who perceive her speech as a reflection of their innermost feelings.

Her success in a field that is always changing has been largely attributed to her ability to combine personal tales with universal themes. Lainey maintains her sense of self by remaining true to herself in a world where fashions in music change with the seasons. Instead of attempting to follow trends or fit into a specific pattern, she allows her experiences to dictate the lyrics. Her songs frequently combine modern production methods and original melodies with traditional country music elements, such as steel guitar and fiddle. A wide range of listeners will find this blend of the old and the contemporary to be both inventive and nostalgic.

For Lainey, making songs serves as a type of therapy in addition to being a creative outlet. She uses music as a coping mechanism and a lens through which to interpret the world when times are hard. Every song she writes is a mirror of her own experience, whether it be about the happiness of reuniting with family or the heartache of a failed love. She also makes her listeners feel less isolated in their challenges by sharing her tale.

Lainey's storytelling style is similar to that of traditional country music icons who came before her. Country music legends like Dolly Parton, Loretta Lynn, and Johnny Cash were adept at using their songs to convey stories about their own and their fans' real-life experiences. Lainey continues this tradition by paying respect to the legends who came before her and infusing contemporary country music with a fresh depth and genuineness.

She follows the tradition of country storytelling, but she also forges her route by incorporating personal and life-relevant themes into her songs. She doesn't hesitate to discuss the specifics of her experiences, whether they involve overcoming obstacles as an adult or growing up in a tiny village. Her storytelling has such an impact because of her desire to be vulnerable in her songs. She knows that a tale becomes more universal the more personal it is.

Lainey's trademark style has evolved into a blend of traditional country components and an intensely intimate narrative. In a field full of gifted artists, it's what makes her stand out. Her music appeals to everyone who has ever suffered, fallen in love, or pursued a dream, not just country music lovers. She freely shares a bit of her soul with the world with every song.

# CHAPTER 4: RISING STAR

## The Release of Her First Album

Lainey Wilson's first record, which represented years of arduous work, tenacity, and everlasting faith in her music, was released at a critical juncture in her life. It was more than simply the release of a song; it was the world's first glimpse into her heart and soul, a bold proclamation that she was prepared to leave her mark in the ferociously competitive country music industry.

She had been putting all of her artistic energy into her songs for years, touring as often as she could and working hard in Nashville's songwriting communities. She was aware that releasing a full-length album would be the real litmus test for her artistic abilities, notwithstanding the little successes along the way. This was her opportunity to exhibit a collection of songs that embodied her identity as a singer-songwriter rather than simply a few standout tracks.

After the publication of her debut album, "Tougher", in 2016, she became well-known in the country music industry. People were drawn in by the honesty that permeated every song, not only the catchy melodies or the well-produced production. "Tougher" was an album that held to Lainey's roots, fusing traditional country sounds with her distinct storytelling flare. It wasn't a compilation of songs designed to fit the mold of commercial success. Each song served a distinct purpose, and when taken as a whole, they created a striking portrait of a young woman with a powerful voice, lofty goals, and a strong sense of self.

"Tougher," the album's title track, became Lainey's anthem. She sang of resiliency, strength, and endurance in it—elements she had learned to embody along the way. Those who could relate to the song's words were drawn to it, especially ladies who had overcome adversity to emerge stronger from it. The song's bold refrain, "I'm tougher than the rest," served as Lainey's motto and a testament to the grit she had accumulated over the years.

"Tougher" featured a number of tracks that showcased Lainey's range as a performer in addition to the album's title track. There were happy songs that praised the small things in life, heartfelt ballads, and everything in between. Her voice, a confident and genuine blend of smokey warmth and pure country soul, brought each song to life. It was obvious that the person who created this album knew exactly who she was and didn't hesitate to be brave or vulnerable.

Although the release of her debut album was an absolute dream, there were difficulties along the way. In such a crowded market, Lainey was still relatively unknown in mainstream country music, so it wasn't easy to get her CD noticed. She had to work even harder to promote her music because no major company was supporting her. She did this by booking gigs anywhere she could and interacting with fans directly on social media. Although the voyage wasn't glamorous, it was evidence of her tenacity and work ethic.

Despite these difficulties, the record started to acquire popularity gradually. Lainey's honesty and genuineness drew in both reviewers and fans, who praised her for being loyal to her origins and creating a sound that was both classic and modern. Although she didn't become famous right away, "Tougher" assisted her in gaining a devoted following of people who valued authentic country music and identified with Lainey's tale.

Observing the effect her songs had on listeners was one of the most satisfying parts of releasing Tougher. After performances, fans would approach Lainey and tell her how a certain song had lifted their spirits during a difficult moment or made them feel understood. That relationship meant everything to Lainey. It motivated her to follow her passion in the first place and validated all the effort she had put into her music.

However, her debut album's release served as a teaching moment as well. Lainey soon discovered that releasing music was only one aspect of a career that required ongoing development and adjustment. "Tougher" was a turning point in her career, but it also laid the groundwork for future developments. She was aware that she couldn't sit back and take it all in; instead, she needed to keep growing as an artist, keep improving her technique, and hold fast to the principles that had brought her this far.

Looking back, Lainey Wilson's "Tougher" the album served as more than simply an album; it was a statement of her independence. It was the moment she formally presented herself to the public, not as a struggling songwriter or Nashville hopeful, but as an artist with a message to convey. She demonstrated with its publication that she could create her imprint without adhering to conventions or trends in the industry. She could achieve her goals with diligence, grit, and a strong emotional bond with the tales she wished to share.

The album didn't have to be a huge hit to be considered successful. For Lainey, it was sufficient that "Tougher" captured every aspect of her journey, including all of her setbacks, triumphs, and life lessons. Furthermore, the groundwork established by her debut album served as a continual reminder of her origins and the principles that shaped her as her career developed.

Lainey would go on to record additional music and achieve even more success in her career in the years that followed. But as the album that got it all started, "Tougher" would always have a particular place in her heart. It was her first public appearance, and she used it to start establishing her special niche in the country music industry.

## Gaining Recognition in the Industry

Lainey Wilson had to fight hard and persevere through a journey of passion, steadfast belief in her talent, and perseverance before she could be recognized in the country music industry. She eventually started to draw attention after years of doing small-scale shows, creating songs late at night, and navigating the erratic Nashville music environment. This wasn't due to her sudden stardom but rather to her consistent, unquestionable development as an artist with something genuine to contribute.

In the world of country music, fame typically develops gradually, and Lainey experienced the same. When she first moved to Nashville, she didn't have the luxury of a major label push or immediate singles. Rather, she forged a way via the daily grind of relentless performances, improving her songwriting and developing real relationships with people in the business. She needed to establish herself not only as a vocalist but also as a storyteller and songwriter who could convey genuineness in each note and lyric.

Lainey's ascent to fame began with a significant turning point when she attracted the interest of influential members of the Nashville songwriting scene. Her honest, emotionally charged songs and striking images immediately distinguished her among the town's plethora of aspirants. She composed songs to express her lived experiences, her inner truths, and her Southern heritage—not merely to make them sound good on the radio. Because of her honesty, record producers and composers ultimately started to view her as more than simply another budding musician.

With her growing reputation in Nashville's close-knit community, Lainey started to have more opportunities to perform. She began performing at prestigious locations, opening for more well-known acts and sharing the stage with performers she had long loved. She started to completely understand the significance of what she was doing at these times when she was in the spotlight in front of ever-increasing audiences. Now, the songs she had composed in her solitary moments reverberated through packed halls, connecting with listeners who could identify with the feelings she infused into each verse.

However, becoming well-known required more than just going to the appropriate events and networking; it required standing out in a field that frequently values consistency over uniqueness. Lainey refused to follow trends or give in to pressure to fit into a certain style because she understood from the start that she wanted to keep her unique sound, which was a mix of traditional country music with a contemporary twist. One of her biggest qualities turned out to be her determination to remain faithful to her artistic individuality. It was evident to both industry insiders and fans that Lainey wasn't only pursuing celebrity but rather producing a body of work that had significance.

The publication of her track "Things a Man Oughta Know" was her big break in the business. The song struck a profound chord with listeners throughout the nation as a sincere meditation on fortitude, independence, and understanding. It was a statement rather than just another catchy song. Although Lainey's work had always been appreciated, this song helped her reach a whole new audience. It quickly rose to the top of the list of songs that country music fans were talking about when radio stations started playing it. It was many listeners' first encounter with Lainey Wilson, and they were captivated by her storytelling skills and genuineness right away.

The success of "Things a Man Oughta Know" also won her praise from critics and other musicians for writing a song that struck a balance between empowerment and vulnerability. It was a song that cut across genre borders, capturing the interest of both younger listeners and die-hard country fans with her unique take on the genre. The song quickly rose to the top of the charts, solidifying Lainey's place among the emerging stars of country music.

Soon after, she received nominations and awards, which cemented her standing in the field. Prestigious groups like the Country Music Association and the Academy of Country Music started to give Lainey recognition. These gestures were a testament to her hard work, her talent to write meaningful songs, and her commitment to remaining true to herself in a field that frequently requires compromise—rather than just a reflection of her rising fame.

However, Lainey's notoriety extended beyond accolades and chart success. It had to do with the respect she received from her colleagues. Her genuineness and inventiveness attracted the attention of other musicians and songwriters, who were keen to collaborate with her. Lainey gained a reputation as someone who was not just gifted but also sincere in a community where reputation and relationships are valued. She became well-liked by many due to her generosity, diligence, and modesty, and she was surrounded by artists who shared her goal and were encouraging.

As her career grew, Lainey found herself sharing stages with some of the biggest names in country music. While on tour with well-known musicians, she had the opportunity to play in front of bigger audiences—many of whom were hearing her music for the first time—and her deep voice, compelling stage presence, and emotional performances won over audiences night after night. Every performance presented an additional chance for her to demonstrate her superiority in the industry.

Even with her increasing notoriety, Lainey never allowed success to alter who she was. She never wavered in her groundedness, never forgetting the years of arduous labor it had taken to get here. Every achievement, be it a number-one hit on the charts, a sold-out performance, or an award nomination, served as a reminder of her progress and her goals. One song at a time, she was pursuing her lifetime passion rather than pursuing popularity for the sake of fame.

# CHAPTER 5: THE BREAKTHROUGH MOMENT

## Hit Singles and Chart Success

A string of hit singles that came in quick succession launched Lainey Wilson into the mainstream and solidified her status as one of the biggest names in country music. Her chart-topping success was the result of her unwavering dedication, distinctive sound, and emotionally charged lyrics, even though her journey to prominence wasn't rapid. Every one of her successful songs was more than simply a statistic on a billboard; it was evidence of her genuineness and her capacity to establish a very intimate connection with her audience.

"Things a Man Oughta Know"'s release was one of her career's biggest turning points. The way this song changed the game. Although Lainey's songwriting had long been appreciated, this specific song elevated her to a prominent position in the country music industry. "Things a Man Oughta Know" touched a nerve with listeners from all walks of life with its potent lyrics on emotional intelligence, self-reliance, and the lessons learned from a difficult background. It was more than simply a song; it was an anthem of vulnerability and inner power, encased in a beautiful country melody that seemed both timeless and modern at the same time.

The song ascended the charts steadily and slowly. It started to gain traction on country radio as fans yearned for something real connected with its message. The song quickly attracted the attention of the larger country music world as it began to receive radio. Lainey's voice had become a mainstay on country music stations throughout the country by the time it peaked at the top of the charts. Not only did "Things a Man Oughta Know" top the Country Airplay chart, but it also marked a turning point in her career and cemented her standing as one of the genre's finest songs.

"Things a Man Oughta Know" was unique not only because of its financial success but also because of Lainey's nuanced portrayal of emotion. Storytelling has always been a key component of country music, and Lainey demonstrated her mastery of the genre with this song. Few songs could have struck listeners as deeply as the way she combined power and vulnerability with a message of what it meant to be really independent. The message of the song was not limited to ladies; men were also drawn to its universal themes of understanding and personal development. This broad appeal contributed to the song's rapid ascent to the top of the charts, where it remained for weeks.

After "Things a Man Oughta Know" became successful, Lainey demonstrated that her breakthrough achievement was not an isolated incident. Her later hits, such as "WWDD" (What Would Dolly Do? ), carried on exhibiting her distinct style of country music, which honored the tradition of the genre while adapting to contemporary tastes. Lainey added her sense of wit and comedy to the lyrics of "WWDD," channeling the wisdom and spirit of country music icon Dolly Parton. Because of its brilliant tribute to one of country music's biggest stars and its infectious hook, the song soon became a fan favorite. It didn't take long for it to land on country charts, enhancing Lainey's reputation as a hitmaker.

The seductive, slow-burning single "Dirty Looks," which revealed a new side of Lainey, was another hit that caused a stir. "Dirty Looks," with its raw, passionate vocals and bluesy overtones, gave audiences a taste of Lainey's flexibility as an artist. She was capable of going beyond the bright, inspiring songs and exploring more profound, personal territory. The song's consistent ascent up the charts was a testament to its widespread popularity, as fans were drawn to Lainey's ability to transition between various themes and moods with ease.

However, Lainey's genuineness may have been more important to her chart success than merely her talent to produce popular songs. Though polished, radio-friendly tracks are frequently prized in this industry, Lainey never lost sight of what made her music special. Her life, her ideals, and her upbringing in rural Louisiana were all reflected in her songs. Her determination to compromise her identity as an artist was evident in every song that shot to the top of the charts.

Lainey's growing prominence was noticed by both industry insiders and fans as her music ascended the charts. Her ability to infuse classic country sounds with a new, contemporary viewpoint made her a genre innovator. She wasn't just another performer trying to make it to the top of the charts; rather, she was a writer of hits who was genuinely moved by the tales she chose to convey via her songs.

Lainey's songs became quite popular on streaming services in addition to her tracks' success on the radio. Millions of people have listened to her music on platforms like Spotify and Apple Music, demonstrating her broad appeal. Through these channels, she was able to reach a worldwide audience, and admirers from other countries came to know and enjoy her music. With every successful single, she got closer to becoming a household name, and her fan base grew every day.

Along with opening doors she had always wanted, Lainey's chart success allowed her to perform on some of the greatest venues in the country music industry. She began opening for well-known bands, attending the Country Music Awards, and headlining her tours as her tracks became more popular. Every performance served as an opportunity to exhibit the same genuineness that had catapulted her songs to the top of the charts, and every number-one hit served as a constant reminder of her progress.

## Collaborations with Other Artists

Lainey Wilson didn't do it alone in her ascent to fame in the country music industry. Collaborations with other artists were essential to extending her reach and securing her place in the industry, even though her voice, songwriting, and genuineness were the key factors that marked her success as an individual. Through these collaborations, she was able to meet new people, experiment with other sounds, and express her viewpoint with musicians from all backgrounds.

One of Lainey's most significant features is the way her collaborations flow organically into her profession. Lainey always treated partnerships as authentic artistic exchanges, even in a business where they can occasionally appear forced or manufactured. Working with both established country music icons and rising singers, she added her unique style to each production, enhancing the song with her distinctive storytelling and strong vocals.

Lainey's collaborations with some of Nashville's most renowned producers and songwriters were a turning point in her career. Songwriters in Nashville frequently get together in rooms to exchange ideas, collaborate on lyrics, and create songs from the ground up. Lainey flourished in these settings, collaborating with writers who had written successes for some of the biggest stars in country music. She kept running into writers in writing rooms who were ready to assist her in realizing her idea. These early joint efforts produced tunes that complemented her voice and benefited from the collective expertise and originality of Nashville's finest.

Lainey collaborated with others on projects other than songwriting. As she became more well-known, she started collaborating directly with musicians, both in and outside of the country genre. A turning moment in her career came when she worked on her first significant project with a fellow country music singer. By collaborating with well-known musicians, she was able to explore new aspects of her talent and reach a wider audience.

One such partnership involved country music icon Jon Pardi. Their duet, "Beer Song," which combined Lainey's contemporary country flair with Jon's classic honky-tonk approach, quickly became a fan favorite. Their vocal chemistry and love of telling stories through music were both on full display in the song. Recognized for his passion for vintage country music, Jon discovered the ideal companion in Lainey, who offered a novel yet empathetic viewpoint. Together, they wrote a tune that appealed to listeners of both modern and traditional country music. Their partnership involved more than just crafting a memorable song; it involved fusing their approaches in a way that honored the diversity of country music's heritage while also looking to the future.

Lainey worked with a variety of musicians, not just country music stars. Her distinct style and approachable lyrics make her a desirable collaborator for performers from various genres. She collaborated with pop and Americana musicians, broadening her musical horizons and introducing her rural upbringing to fresh listeners. Through these cross-genre collaborations, she was able to explore a variety of sounds, which stimulated her creativity and forced her to venture beyond her comfort zone. Lainey demonstrated that she could compete in any musical setting while staying true to her roots in country music.

Her work with the hit-making team of Hardy and Morgan Wallen was one of the highlights of her joint endeavors. Hardy and Wallen, both rising talents in their own right, infused their music with a gritty, rebellious attitude that went well with Lainey's mix of brave personality and honest storytelling. Fans were taken aback by their unexpected collaboration on the eerie ballad "Wait in the Truck," which explores themes of justice and retribution. The song's gloomy storyline was in stark contrast to some of Lainey's previous compositions, but it also demonstrated her versatility. The popularity of the song further demonstrated Lainey's versatility as an artist, and there was an obvious chemistry between her and her collaborators.

Lainey's involvement in live performances and special events demonstrated her ability to collaborate with musicians of all genres. She frequently received invitations to participate in festivals, charity concerts, and award events with other country music celebrities. She was able to connect with other performers and show off her charismatic stage presence during these performances. In addition to being a platform for performance, sharing the stage with some of the biggest stars in country music offered the ability to network and build enduring ties within the business.

One aspect of Lainey's collaborative journey did not change: she is real. She never forgot who she was as an artist, whether she was co-writing a song with a pop star or singing a duet with a country music icon. Her voice always came through, both literally and figuratively, making sure that the finished product felt like a true representation of her artistic identity regardless of who she collaborated with.

Lainey's partnerships were, in many respects, a logical progression of her fundamental conviction in the potency of narrative. She understood that everyone had a story to tell, and through working with other artists, she discovered fresh avenues for telling those tales. Every joint effort provided her with the chance to combine her voice with another's and produce something fresh and significant that neither could have done on their own. These collaborations were about more than just penning great songs; they were also about developing relationships, sharing knowledge, and developing as artists.

# CHAPTER 6: THE HEART OF THE FANS

## Building a Dedicated Fanbase

It took more for Lainey Wilson to develop a devoted following than merely putting out successful music and gaining radio play. It was all about forging a sincere bond with her listeners, sharing profoundly felt tales, and exhibiting the kind of genuineness that gives followers the impression that they are speaking with her face-to-face. Lainey recognized the importance of her fans early in her career and made a concerted effort to build a relationship with them that went beyond just music.

Lainey's upbringing in a rural town informed her strategy for gaining followers. She was taught the value of community while growing up in Baskin, Louisiana, where people helped one another and built connections based on mutual respect and trust. She carried that mindset with her when she ventured into the country music industry. She let her admirers come to her organically and concentrated on being herself rather than attempting to please everyone. She had no desire to put on a front or change into someone she wasn't in order to win people over. She thought that if she remained authentic, the proper people would discover her music.

During the initial phases of her profession, Lainey traveled and performed in intimate settings such as pubs and tiny theaters, where her fans could directly experience the intensity of her performance. She was able to engage the audience in these small spaces in a manner that larger venues were unable to. She engaged with the audience, telling jokes and sharing anecdotes in between songs, giving everyone a sense of being a part of something unique. She didn't just play for the audience. People left her live concerts feeling as though they had acquired a new friend in Lainey, in addition to being amazed by her talent. This became a major component of Lainey's fan base-building efforts.

Many people were moved by her humble background and down-to-earth demeanor, especially those who lived in rural areas and could relate to her music because it mirrored their own experiences. Lainey's songs resonated with individuals from all walks of life because they highlighted tales of perseverance, heartache, and personal development. Fans found solace and inspiration in her words, whether she was singing about the challenges of daily life, her birthplace, or the lessons she had learned along the road. People kept returning for more because of her strong emotional connection, curious to hear what she had to say next.

As social media emerged as a vital instrument for performers to engage with their audience base, Lainey adopted it completely, albeit uniquely. Content that felt polished, carefully chosen, and remote didn't appeal to her. Rather, she provided fans with a behind-the-scenes glimpse at her life, including the highs and lows, via apps like Instagram and TikTok. She would offer glimpses into her songwriting process, humorous anecdotes from her travels, and reflective thoughts on her experience. Her openness was greatly welcomed by the audience, who felt that they were getting to know Lainey Wilson beyond her theatrical presence.

Lainey gained such a devoted fan base in part because of her constant presence. She didn't simply vanish in the time between tours and album releases. Whether via social media updates, live streaming, or unexpected acoustic performances, she made it a point to stay in touch with her supporters. Her admirers were ferociously devoted to her after realizing how much she cared for them and helped her along the journey. They were there, eager to listen and share whenever she put out new music. They got tickets for her upcoming tour and brought their pals along. She never took for granted this sense of loyalty, which was essential to her success.

Lainey made it a point to express her gratitude to her followers in meaningful ways as her career flourished. Regardless of how exhausted she was, she would frequently stop by to greet fans following performances, sign autographs, and take photos. She realized the significance of these exchanges surpassed only that of the music itself. The chance to finally meet Lainey in person cemented their bond with a lot of her admirers. She was more than simply a voice on the radio; she was a person who genuinely cared about them and took the time to show them that they were valued and seen.

Word-of-mouth also helped Lainey's fan base grow. Her admirers turned into her strongest supporters, posting about her performances on social media and recommending her music to friends and family. People quickly fell in love with her because of her contagious personality and sincere attitude, and her following base quickly expanded beyond the typical country music audience. Her songs drew in listeners who weren't usually into country music because of the captivating tales and strong emotions she conveyed.

Along with her community work, Lainey's ascent in the business contributed to the growth of her fan following. More people started to pay attention as she started receiving acclaim from award programs, radio stations, and other artists. She never forgot about her early supporters, though, even as her fan base expanded. Knowing that her core fan group was the cornerstone of her success, she persisted in carving out time for them.

Lainey has always focused on fostering a feeling of community in her approach to fan interaction. She wants her fans to feel like they are a part of a community and are traveling with her, not simply as her audience. Lainey has consistently given her audience a sense of value, whether it is via a moving song or a cordial conversation following a performance. Because of this, she has a sizable and fervently loyal fan base that is committed to whatever she does.

## Engaging with Her Audience

One of the things that has made Lainey Wilson stand out in the country music industry is her ability to interact with her audience. Her ability to connect with people goes beyond just her music; instead of viewing her followers as cold admirers, she treats them as friends and fellow travelers. She has developed this close bond from her early musical days, and it is still the main factor in her success.

Lainey creates an environment that feels less like a concert and more like a get-together of old friends from the time she walks onto the stage. No matter how big the gathering, she always manages to make her listeners feel heard and noticed. Whether performing in a crowded arena or a tiny, private setting, Lainey has a talent for adding a personal touch to each show. People feel as if they are sharing a moment with someone who genuinely cares about their experience rather than just witnessing a show, thanks to her genuine warmth and down-to-earth charm.

Lainey's narrative is a major factor in her ability to connect with her audience. She weaves personal meaning into every song she performs, and she spends time during her performances sharing the backstories of her songs. She frequently gives fans a peek into her life, thoughts, and feelings by sharing the idea behind a new song before dropping the bass. The performance feels more intimate and personal as a result of her moments of vulnerability, which enable the audience to relate to her on a deeper level. After one of her performances, fans have the impression that they know more about the artist than just the song.

One of the main factors in Lainey's audience involvement is her sense of humor. She is well-known for her sharp tongue and lighthearted banter, which enable her to connect with the audience easily. Lighthearted comedy abounds throughout her performances as she teases her teammates and cracks jokes about life on the road. Her fans feel comfortable with her and are encouraged to engage with her throughout the concert because of her approachability. Lainey frequently engages in lighthearted banter with her audience, answers enthusiastic yells, and extends her gratitude to supporters who have come a long way to witness her performance. These exchanges give each performance a distinct, impromptu flavor that reflects her lively nature.

Lainey maintains a deep and intimate interaction with her audience even when she is not on stage. Although she doesn't utilize social media in the conventional, controlled manner that many artists do, it has become one of her favorite tools for keeping in touch with her followers. Rather, Lainey lets her fans into every aspect of her daily life, including anything from her coffee ritual in the morning to her behind-the-scenes tour experiences. She provides an intimate look into her life outside of the spotlight by sharing videos of herself having fun with friends, creating new music, or grooving to her favorite tunes. In a day of flawlessly manicured online personalities, this kind of genuineness is uncommon, and her fans greatly value it.

Her live Q&A sessions also demonstrate Lainey's intention to interact directly with her audience. Fans may ask her anything during her frequent Q&A sessions on social media sites like Instagram and TikTok, including questions about her favorite songs and opinions on current affairs. Lainey gives fans an opportunity to witness her genuine personality in action during these sessions, where her comments are both amusing and poignant. The most remarkable thing about her is the thoughtfulness with which she responds to fan queries, giving each one a sense of importance. For an artist of her caliber, this kind of engagement is uncommon, and it has only strengthened her followers' devotion to her.

Whenever feasible, Lainey tries to meet her fans when she's on tour. She spends time taking photos, interacting with fans, and signing autographs following a lot of her performances. For Lainey, these aren't just about getting attention; they're also about forging genuine bonds with those who encourage her. Her genuine appreciation is evident as she remembers individuals, inquires about their life and expresses gratitude for their attendance. These exchanges create a deep impression and have assisted her in building a fan community that feels like a family. Supporters are aware that Lainey sees them as more than just ticket purchasers.

Lainey writes songs with the same commitment to interacting with her listeners. Her interactions with fans, the stories they tell her, and the experiences they have had all serve as inspiration for many of her songs. She pays close attention to what her fans have to say and frequently incorporates their experiences into her new compositions. As a result, Lainey's followers feel as though they are a part of the creative process and share a common experience. Since they know that a new song she publishes might have been influenced by something they've shared with her, her fans frequently feel a personal connection to it.

Most importantly, Lainey's genuine affection for her followers is what fuels her audience engagement. She has always known that the people who support her music and believe in her are what makes her successful in addition to her talent. Whether it's a moving performance, a humorous social media message, or a private chat following a show, Lainey never fails to remind her fans how much she values them. She is now regarded as one of the most adored country music musicians because of her sincerity.

Lainey believes that connecting with her audience is about more than just entertaining them; it's about creating enduring bonds. She never takes for granted the fact that she is able to live her dream because she is aware of her fans. Her appreciation for all of the people who have helped her along the journey is evident in every song she creates, every show she puts on, and every conversation she has with her fans. Lainey Wilson's authentic relationship with her followers has aided in the development of both a community and a successful career.

# CHAPTER 7: LIFE ON THE ROAD

## Touring Experiences

Lainey Wilson's rise to prominence in the country music industry has coincided with equally transformational and exciting touring experiences. These experiences have greatly influenced Lainey's artistic development and her relationship with her fans, which have ranged from small-town performances to sharing the stage with some of the country's biggest artists. Every tour has presented its own set of lessons, difficulties, and triumphant moments, and Lainey has seized every chance to develop herself.

It was anything from glamorous when Lainey first began touring. Her reality was hustling from gig to gig, playing at county fairs, tiny bars, and honky-tonks while traveling in cramped vans with her band. Her goal in going on these early tours was to establish her name from the bottom up, not to become famous or wealthy. Even though she occasionally performed for small audiences of only a few dozen people, Lainey gave it her best. She approached every gig as though it were at the Grand Ole Opry, whether it was a neighborhood festival or a dive bar in the middle of nowhere.

Lainey's modest beginnings gave her the opportunity to cultivate a work ethic and tenacity that would aid her when she moved up to bigger stages and longer tours. Although the journey wasn't always smooth, it did teach her how to deal with the monotony of nonstop travel, erratic timetables, and the mental and physical strain of being on tour. Her early experiences also influenced her as a performer, teaching her to adjust, develop, and become adept at engaging audiences in every situation.

As Lainey's career developed, she was able to take advantage of more lucrative touring possibilities, such as opening for well-known country music bands. It was humble and thrilling to share the stage with performers she had long respected. It allowed her to see directly how larger-scale tours functioned and what it took to enthrall thousands of people. Her understanding of the nuances of stage production, the significance of timing during a set, and the creation of memorable moments that would stay with viewers long after the play concluded were all greatly aided by these experiences.

For Lainey, seeing and interacting with fans in person has been one of the most fulfilling parts of touring. The excitement of live performances has always fueled her love for touring—feeling the audience sing along to her songs and witnessing people being impacted by her music on an emotional level. She frequently discusses the excitement of doing live performances, as no two are ever the same. Every tour is an adventure because of the unpredictable energy of the crowd and the distinct atmosphere of each location.

Her touring experiences have further increased her ability to interact and establish a connection with her audience. On stage, Lainey's genuine demeanor comes through as she never hesitates to engage with the audience directly, share personal anecdotes, and have sincere conversations. She can captivate an audience with an intimate acoustic performance or a big band rock show by involving them in the experience and making them feel like they're a part of something unique. Lainey's admirers frequently leave her performances with the impression that they have a personal connection with her, and this sense of unity has been essential in growing her devoted following.

Lainey has had the opportunity to tour the nation and see more of her varied fan base, which has helped her understand them better. She has given performances in both large and small locales, at intimate settings, and at large festivals, each with its distinct audience. She has been able to observe firsthand via these experiences how different individuals connect with her songs and how fans of country music come from all walks of life. Her wide range of touring experiences has impacted her songwriting, as she finds inspiration in the people and locations she encounters along the route.

Lainey has performed with country music icons on a number of high-profile tours and festivals as her career has grown. She has been able to share the stage with musicians she has always listened to and admired from a distance, thanks to these events, which have made her dreams come true. It has been strange and rewarding to play at legendary locations like Nashville's Ryman Auditorium or significant country music events like Stagecoach or CMA Fest. Lainey frequently thinks back on her path from small-town stages to career-defining performances during these times.

Of course, traveling has its share of difficulties. Constant travel, late nights, and early mornings can be physically taxing on the body. However, Lainey has always treated the grind of touring with the same tenacity and resolve that she applies to her songwriting. She is driven despite the demanding schedule because she recognizes that every night she spends on stage is a chance to interact with her audience. Although being a touring artist is not for everyone, Lainey has accepted this lifestyle fully since she believes that the benefits of performing live far exceed the pdrawbacks.

Staying connected to her roots has been a priority for Lainey throughout her traveling career. She has always brought a little bit of Baskin, Louisiana, with her when she travels, regardless of the distance she has covered or the size of the venues. Her admirers connect with her authenticity—her capacity to remain loyal to who she is and where she came from—and her performances come off as sincere and emotional.

## Balancing Fame and Personal Life

Lainey Wilson's personal life has become more complicated to manage as her profile has grown in the country music industry. An artist's life can be quickly consumed by the frenzy of recording, traveling, and public appearances; this frequently results in a struggle to retain a sense of normalcy. Lainey, on the other hand, has tackled this task with a blend of tenacity, genuineness, and a dedication to remaining loyal to herself.

Strong identification is the foundation of Lainey's capacity to manage her newfound stardom. She is aware that despite the success of her work, she is still the same person that she was in the background. Her upbringing in Baskin, Louisiana, gave her a strong sense of self-worth and a close-knit family dynamic that acts as a stabilizing force. Lainey frequently considers the importance of her family to her sense of self, highlighting how they keep her anchored in the middle of the upheaval of her professional life. Frequent family get-togethers, whether they are intimate meals or elaborate festivities, give her the love and support she needs to deal with the challenges of celebrity.

Lainey prioritizes taking time for herself and her loved ones despite the pressures of her profession. Rather than being shown in large gestures, this dedication is instead shown in modest, deliberate moments. She treasures peaceful nights at home, for example, when she can decompress and forget about the demands of her public life. She can refuel during these quiet times of introspection and seclusion, which guarantees that she will approach her task with fresh vitality and inventiveness. Her mental health and general well-being depend on this balance, which also allows her to keep making music that connects with listeners.

Lainey understands the need to preserve her friendships outside of the music business as well. Her close group of acquaintances from her hometown provides her a feeling of comfort and normalcy. These connections, which serve as a constant reminder of her origins, are based on mutual support, humor, and shared experiences. Lainey emphasizes how important it is for her to find time for phone calls and in-person meetings because they keep her centered and connected to who she really is. These friendships serve as a constant reminder to her of the little pleasures in life and the value of spending time with the people she cares about when the demands of celebrity start to get to her.

In Lainey's search for balance, social media has evolved into both a tool and a challenge. She can interact with fans and share her songs on social media sites like Instagram and Twitter. Still, there may be a blurring of the boundaries between her personal and professional lives. Lainey is cautious about the information she posts online, trying to preserve her privacy and be genuine at the same time. Whether it's an open moment from the road or an enjoyable day spent with friends, she frequently posts glimpses of her life on social media, but she takes care not to overshare or reveal personal information. She may develop a sincere relationship with her audience while maintaining the privacy of the most intimate parts of her life thanks to this deliberate approach.

Managing relationships in the public eye can be especially difficult. Lainey has been open about the challenges of dating while in the spotlight, pointing out that it can be challenging to find someone aware of the particular demands and expectations of her line of work.

She yet maintains her faith in love and cherishes candid communication in her partnerships. Lainey is aware that the ideal companion will push her to put her happiness and well-being first in addition to supporting her aspirations. This viewpoint enables her to pursue her goals and cultivate deep connections while preserving a feeling of balance between her personal and professional lives.

The unpredictable nature of the music business complicates Lainey's life. Due to unanticipated events, shifting schedules, and the need for flexibility, she's become robust and adaptive. She may manage the inevitable ups and downs in her job by adopting an adaptable mindset and never losing focus on the things that really matter—her relationships and well-being. Lainey frequently stresses that obstacles are a part of the process and that keeping an optimistic mindset is essential to juggling the demands of celebrity with her own goals.

Lainey Wilson has maintained a lifestyle that values connection, sincerity, and balance despite everything. She is well aware that, although playing country music plays a big role in her life, it does not define her in the slightest. Lainey conquers the obstacles of celebrity with elegance and tenacity by staying true to herself, appreciating her relationships, and accepting the help of her family and friends. Her dedication to striking a balance between her fulfillment and her career aspirations is evidence of her resilience as a person and as an artist, guaranteeing that she can live a glamorous life while adhering to her core principles.

Lainey's method is unique in an industry where artists are frequently under pressure to live up to predetermined standards. In addition to being a rising star in the country music industry, she values her life off the stage. Her story is an example to others, showing them that it's possible to follow one's passions and still value relationships, personal development, and self-care.

# CHAPTER 8: ADVOCACY AND IMPACT

## Using Her Platform for Change

Lainey Wilson stands out as an outspoken supporter of change in her town and beyond at a time when artists are realizing the power of their platforms. Her dedication to making a significant effect with her music and public presence demonstrates a profound awareness of her duty as an artist in the twenty-first century. Lainey has used her increasing prominence to raise awareness of crucial topics, support underrepresented voices, and motivate her followers to make constructive changes rather than just basking in the perks of fame.

Lainey's commitment to advocacy stems from her upbringing in Baskin, Louisiana, as well as her own experiences and principles. She was raised in a close-knit community and saw firsthand the difficulties that many families encounter, such as problems with poverty, access to healthcare, and education. These events affected her worldview and her ambition to bring about change. She is conscious that her platform as a well-known singer gives her a special potential to spread awareness of these important social issues and motivate action.

Mental health awareness is one of the most important subjects that Lainey advocates for. Acknowledging the stigma associated with mental health issues, she candidly discusses her difficulties with anxiety and the demands of celebrity. Lainey encourages her fans to prioritize their mental health and seek help when necessary by being open and honest about these subjects. She routinely shares groups that offer information and help on social media to raise awareness of mental health options. Lainey's openness and vulnerability regarding her challenges strike a deep chord with her audience, encouraging empathy and a sense of connection among individuals who might otherwise feel alone in their circumstances.

She also supports women's empowerment in the music industry, where gender inequality is still a major problem. She is a vocal advocate for the issues that female artists confront, such as underrepresentation, uneven compensation, and the need for more encouraging settings in the business. She motivates a new generation of female musicians to follow their aspirations despite any difficulties they may face by using her platform to bring attention to these concerns. Lainey frequently works with other female musicians to elevate their voices and spread the idea that women in the music industry should be honored and encouraged.

Lainey is dedicated to giving back to the community in ways that go beyond the music business. She regularly takes part in fundraising activities and charitable events, giving her time and money to assist regional causes. Lainey recognizes the value of giving back to the community that reared her, whether it be through engaging in programs to improve education for impoverished children, helping at shelters, or donating to food banks. She invites her supporters to become engaged as well, and her actions show that she genuinely wants to make a positive difference. She instills in her audience a sense of social awareness and responsibility by imitating this behavior.

Furthermore, Lainey has actively addressed societal topics through her music. In addition to showcasing her narrative skills, songs like "Things a Man Oughta Know" also contain messages about relationships and self-worth that a lot of listeners can relate to. She is aware that music can be an effective medium for reflecting on oneself and making societal commentary. She establishes a bond with her listeners that goes beyond mere amusement by incorporating themes of resilience and empowerment into her songs. Lainey's skill at incorporating these ideas into her songs shows that she is aware of the influence that music may have on listeners' lives.

Lainey's influence is growing along with her profession. She has been asked to take part in talks and panels about the direction of country music, where she promotes diversity and inclusivity in the genre. By being in these places, Lainey not only makes her voice heard but also invites others to participate in the discussion. Her dedication to utilizing her position to promote conversation about significant issues has established her as a renowned personality in the field and among her peers.

She now uses social media as a vital tool in her advocacy work. Through social media sites like Twitter and Instagram, where she offers her opinions on a range of topics and motivates her followers to take action, she successfully engages her audience. Lainey utilizes her online platform to spread good change, whether she is endorsing a humanitarian organization or advocating for mental health awareness. Her fans connect with her sincerity and relatability, which amplifies the impact and accessibility of her teachings.

Lainey Wilson is refreshing and motivating because she is willing to speak up and use her platform for change in a world where many artists choose to keep quiet about contentious matters. Her dedication to promoting women's emancipation, mental health, and community assistance indicates a profound awareness of her obligation as an artist. Lainey understands that the chance to affect, uplift, and leave a lasting impression on the world around her comes along with celebrity.

## Community Involvement and Philanthropy

Lainey Wilson's career in the music business has been distinguished not just by her creative achievements but also by her steadfast dedication to charitable giving and community service. Lainey has prioritized giving back in meaningful ways because she understands the tremendous influence music can have on people and communities. This is a reflection of her conviction in the strength of support and collective action.

She has always been acutely conscious of her roots in Baskin, Louisiana, and the struggles that many people in her community and beyond experience. She felt obligated to help others in need as a result of this understanding, and she has actively looked for ways to get involved in her community. Lainey is a living example of connection and giving, whether it is through her time helping or her donation of show money.

Lainey has made a significant impact in the community by volunteering for numerous nonprofits and charities. She frequently takes part in fundraising events for mental health programs, children in need, and impoverished families. Lainey utilizes her platform to mobilize support for issues that align with her values because she thinks that even tiny actions may have a big impact. She engages her followers and invites them to support her in changing the world through food drives and fundraising events. Her fans develop a sense of camaraderie as a result of her community involvement, which turns her fan base into a powerful force for good.

Lainey has made it a point to support national and international initiatives that demonstrate her commitment to social justice and equality in addition to her local endeavors. She has advocated for causes like access to education, mental health awareness, and the value of helping underprivileged areas. Lainey amplifies the messages of these organizations and inspires her audience to take action by partnering with them. Her support goes beyond simple endorsement; she actively takes part in campaigns aimed at confronting these issues head-on.

Her charitable endeavors are not limited to her music. Understanding the powerful effects that music can have on connection and healing, she has used her artistic abilities to raise money for a variety of organizations by taking part in benefit concerts and charity albums. These performances are a potent reminder of the ability of art to uplift and connect people in addition to showcasing her talent. Her readiness to contribute her voice and resources to these kinds of projects is indicative of her conviction that artists have a special duty to uplift their communities via their creations.

Lainey is a philanthropist who is especially notable for her dedication to youth empowerment. Recognizing the difficulties young people in her neighborhood experience, she often interacts with educational institutions and mentorship programs. Lainey encourages the next generation of artists to follow their ambitions and embrace their creativity by giving talks and workshops. She places a strong emphasis on education and self-expression, acknowledging that young people navigating their issues might find a transformational outlet in the arts.

She encourages her followers to support causes that share her values by using her social media platform to promote charity efforts. She encourages her audience to take action by bringing attention to causes she supports and providing information about these organizations. Her followers are drawn to her genuine style and value her openness and dedication to changing the world. By participating, she not only strengthens her relationship with her audience but also gives them the confidence to get involved in charitable endeavors themselves.

Lainey Wilson is a prime example of the significant influence a musician can have off the stage because of her charitable work and involvement in the community. Her commitment to giving back reflects her strong sense of duty and her wish to make the world a better place. Lainey encourages people to see their potential for change by using her platform for good, creating a culture of empathy and support that knows no bounds.

# CHAPTER 9: PERSONAL STRUGGLES AND TRIUMPHS

## Navigating Challenges Behind the Scenes

Though poignant lyrics and captivating melodies have contributed to Lainey Wilson's climb to popularity, the road behind the scenes has been complex. Similar to numerous artists, Lainey has encountered numerous obstacles that are frequently concealed from the general public. Overcoming these obstacles has not only put her perseverance to the test. Still, it has also molded her into the person and artist she is today, impacting the music and message she produces.

Given how fiercely competitive the music business is, Lainey soon discovered that more than skill is required to ensure success. She was immediately faced with the realities of a crowded industry full of wannabe musicians vying for listeners' attention. Lainey frequently had to remind herself of her distinct voice and vision within the cacophony of this fierce competition, which may be intimidating. She experienced times of worry and self-doubt, wondering if her ambitions would come true or if she would be another lost artist in the shuffle.

Lainey's battle to define her identity as an artist was one of the biggest obstacles she had to overcome. She faced pressure to live up to industry expectations as she moved from her Louisiana origins to the larger country music scene. Artists may experience pressure to live up to the expectations of record labels and producers, who frequently have a particular sound in mind. Lainey faced the difficult task of staying authentic while simultaneously discovering a means to connect with a larger audience. She had to strike a balance between her music and artistic vision, which frequently resulted in restless nights full of worry and reflection.

Obstacles related to money also affected her early career. Lainey had to face the realities of supporting her passion, just like a lot of up-and-coming musicians do. Because it takes a lot of money to tour, record, and promote music, she frequently found herself in tight financial difficulties. She occasionally had to make compromises due to her financial situation, such as taking on more jobs to fund her singing career. Although juggling many obligations and working to establish her brand was a demanding process, it gave her a strong work ethic and a sense of resolve that would serve her well in the future.

Lainey maneuvered through the complexities of industry networking behind the scenes. Establishing connections with influential people, fellow artists, and industry professionals is essential for success, but it can also provide difficulties. While trying to break into established circles, Lainey frequently felt like an outsider and recognized the value of teamwork. She had to be strong and brave in order to make relationships because she was going to be rejected and disappointed. But she also learned a lot from these experiences about tenacity and the value of being genuine in relationships.

The demands of celebrity also increased as Lainey's popularity grew. Artists' public personas are frequently the subject of criticism and examination. Lainey had to learn how to manage the pressures of her work and her personal life while navigating the complications of being in the spotlight. She began to yearn for the ease of her previous days because the continuous attention might make her feel alone. Her music developed a theme of her effort to strike a balance between her private and public lives, which helped her connect with people who felt the same way.

In addition, Lainey had to continually manage her mental well-being in the face of her professional obligations. She frequently has to put coping mechanisms in place because touring, recording, and performing can be extremely stressful. After realizing that taking care of herself was crucial to maintaining her love of music, Lainey started advocating for self-care.

Her songwriting was influenced by her journey of prioritizing her mental health, which helped her create lyrics that spoke to people going through comparable experiences.

Equipped with the knowledge gained from her struggles, Lainey Wilson has become a strong force in the country music industry despite everything. The hardships she overcame behind the scenes have enhanced her artistic sensibility, and her viewpoint is both inspiring and accessible. Lainey has decided to accept her hardships rather than run from them, allowing them to inspire her art and help her establish a stronger connection with her audience.

## Overcoming Obstacles in Her Career

Lainey Wilson's rise to prominence in the country music industry has been nothing short of extraordinary, but it hasn't been without challenges. These difficulties—from personal hardships to industry expectations—have molded her resilience and sculpted her craft, allowing her to turn setbacks into opportunities for growth.

Making her voice heard in a very competitive industry was one of Lainey's biggest early career setbacks. When she first started performing in Nashville, she soon discovered that a lot of excellent musicians are frequently overlooked. Lainey had to come up with unique strategies to stand out from the crowd of hopefuls fighting for the same possibilities. Instead of giving in to what other people thought she should be like, she embraced her uniqueness. Lainey concentrated on perfecting her craft and creating her distinct sound, which blended classic country elements with a contemporary touch. She started to carve out her own space in the congested market by remaining loyal to her heritage while experimenting with her sound.

Another major obstacle in Lainey's path was money. She encountered the harsh reality of financial uncertainty, particularly in the early going, just like many other budding performers. The expense of touring can be high, and musicians frequently need help to make ends meet due to the unpredictability of music industry revenue. Lainey had to make difficult choices concerning investments in her music career on a number of occasions. These experiences made her realize the need for preparation and financial literacy, which encouraged her to look for partnerships and sponsorships that would lessen the strain. Her persistence paid off as she eventually established herself and was able to concentrate more on her passion than just getting by.

The difficulty Lainey faced in conquering gender prejudice in a field dominated by men was another significant barrier. Male musicians have traditionally dominated the country music scene, and women frequently encounter more discrimination and obstacles. Lainey was resolved not to allow anything to stop her. She started to speak out in favor of women in country music, highlighting the value of diversity and representation with her platform. In addition to elevating herself, Lainey blazed the path for upcoming generations of female artists by standing by her fellow female artists and taking part in activities that promote female empowerment. Her work has aided in the expansion of a movement aimed at dispelling myths and giving other voices in the genre a platform.

Personal issues have significantly shaped Lainey's career. It has frequently been difficult for her to strike a balance between the responsibilities of her work and her personal life. There was little time for friends and family because of her busy traveling schedule and relentless efforts to promote her songs. It can be challenging for artists to maintain a sense of normalcy as a result of this separation because it can cause emotions of loneliness and isolation. Lainey discovered how to put her mental health first by defining boundaries, scheduling specific time for self-care, and spending quality time with her loved ones. Her dedication to preserving her health not only made her more resilient but also gave her music a more genuine emotional depth.

The pressure to be successful and uphold a public image has also brought with it a unique set of difficulties. Expectations from the business and her fan base increased in tandem with Lainey's rising profile. There were moments when Lainey struggled with worry and self-doubt because of the immense pressure to provide chart-topping tunes and fascinating performances constantly. She resorted to her craft, expressing her feelings through songwriting, to counter this. She found that writing gave her a therapeutic way to explore her emotions and experiences. Her reflective approach not only helped her deal with the demands of celebrity, but it also struck a chord with her followers, who took comfort in her songs.

Lainey Wilson has shown herself to be a master of resilience in the face of difficulty. Every challenge she has faced has acted as a spur to her development and advanced her on her path. She has turned her failures into moving stories that inspire her fans and influence her music instead of letting them define her. Lainey's story serves as a powerful reminder of the value of tenacity, showing us that obstacles in the way of achievement are frequently surmountable with willpower, ingenuity, and a steadfast dedication to one's work.

# CHAPTER 10: THE FUTURE OF COUNTRY MUSIC

## Lainey's Vision for the Genre

With a distinct vision to reinvent the genre for a new generation, Lainey Wilson is leading the way in a momentous moment in country music. Lainey's viewpoint is both novel and vital in an industry that frequently struggles with the conflict between respecting its history and embracing innovation. She has roots in classic country music but keeps her eyes firmly focused on the future. Authenticity, inclusivity, and a dedication to delivering stories that connect with listeners from all backgrounds define her vision.

Lainey's concept is based on her conviction that real storytelling has great power. She views country music as a means of expressing genuine feelings and experiences rather than merely polished production and catchy hooks. Lainey aims to compose music that touches on all facets of the human experience, including happiness, heartache, resiliency, and everything in between. She establishes a stronger connection with her listeners by incorporating personal stories into her songs. This emphasis on genuineness opens the door for artists to explore a variety of issues and viewpoints by pushing the genre to go beyond clichés and embrace the complexity of life.

Another essential component of Lainey's concept is inclusivity. She is aware that embracing voices from many origins and expanding the genre's reach is essential to the future of country music. Lainey aggressively advocates for the notion that country music ought to be a welcoming genre for people of all backgrounds, genders, and races. She works with musicians from different genres and supports other female musicians, aiming to obfuscate the boundaries that have traditionally separated the music industry. By doing this, she enhances her creative output and promotes a more varied and inclusive music scene that better captures the complexity of contemporary society.

In addition to supporting progress, Lainey's vision includes a great regard for the genre's historical foundations. She continues to be inspired by the pioneers of country music and respects their contributions. But respecting tradition, in her opinion, does not imply adhering to it. Rock, pop, and Americana are just a few of the styles Lainey isn't afraid to try out in her music. In addition to keeping her work current and interesting, this blending of genres encourages listeners who might not otherwise be drawn to country music to give it a try. Lainey maintains the vibrancy and energy of country music by acting as a link between the classic and modern.

Lainey also sees an artistic community where people help one another rather than compete with one another. Artists may feel alone at times due to the competitive nature of the music business, but Lainey actively seeks to alter that perception. She promotes cooperation above competition, calling for musicians to unite in order to create and support one another. She thinks that by encouraging a sense of unity, the genre as a whole may gain and create more inventive, richer music that represents a shared vision.

Lainey's dedication to her goal is evident in her work and the relationships she builds in the business; it is not just an aspirational commitment. As she rises, she never wavers from her goal of honoring the history of country music and moving it forward. Her genuineness and enthusiasm strike a chord with both fans and other musicians, positioning her as a key figure in the genre's continuous development.

When considering the future of country music, Lainey Wilson serves as an example of the possibilities for development and evolution in a genre that depends heavily on narrative and emotional resonance. In addition to blazing her trail, she encourages others to follow suit by supporting genuineness, inclusivity, and teamwork in the creation of a dynamic and varied music scene.

## Mentoring the Next Generation of Artists

Along with focusing on her ascent to prominence, Lainey Wilson has made a name for herself in the country music industry by encouraging others. As a rising celebrity, she is committed to mentoring the next generation of musicians and is aware of the difficulties that budding artists encounter. Her dedication to mentoring others demonstrates her faith in the strength of the community and the value of encouraging those who choose to follow in her footsteps.

Lainey's approach to coaching stems from her own experiences negotiating the music business. Having gone through many obstacles herself, she is aware of the uncertainty and challenges that come with pursuing a career in music. Lainey frequently tells her narrative to aspiring artists, highlighting the values she has discovered in tenacity, sincerity, and remaining loyal to one's ideas. She not only inspires people by sharing details of her trip, but she also offers helpful advice that can help them steer clear of some of the same mistakes she made.

Building confidence in up-and-coming artists is one of Lainey's main goals as a mentor. She stresses how crucial it is to have confidence in oneself and one's voice. Self-doubt is a common problem for young artists, particularly in a field that is cutthroat and subject to severe criticism. Lainey encourages her mentees to embrace their uniqueness and share their tales, actively working to build in them a feeling of self-worth. She contributes to the development of a new generation of artists who are fearless in expressing themselves by reiterating the notion that their experiences are worthwhile and legitimate.

Apart from enhancing self-assurance, Lainey is committed to providing useful advice during the music composition process. She frequently shares her songwriting methods and creative process at workshops and unofficial jam sessions. She fosters experimentation and collaboration by sharing her creative space with others, fostering an atmosphere that is conducive to the success of budding artists. Lainey cultivates a culture where ideas can flow freely, resulting in creative and genuine music, because she feels that teamwork is essential to growth.

Beyond just music, Lainey also mentors people in their career and personal growth. She promotes mental health awareness in her conversations with mentees because she recognizes that the artist's journey may be emotionally stressful. Lainey stresses the value of striking a balance between a person's personal and professional life in her encouragement of aspiring musicians to take care of their mental health. Through her attention to these frequently neglected facets, she provides prospective artists with the means to manage the demands of the business.

Lainey is also a strong supporter of inclusion in country music. Understanding that representation in the industry is important, she regularly mentors female artists as well as artists from a variety of backgrounds. By elevating marginalized voices, she contributes to a more varied musical landscape that represents the range of experiences within the genre. Lainey thinks that by supporting one another, the music business as a whole may gain from a variety of viewpoints, producing more meaningful and relatable songs.

Lainey is dedicated to her duty as a mentor, even as she forges ahead on her own. She is aware that other people's success depends on her own, and she takes great satisfaction in serving as an inspiration to those who are just starting. By serving as a mentor, Lainey helps artists feel a feeling of connection and belonging and lets them know they're not traveling alone.

For the upcoming generation of musicians, Lainey Wilson represents a ray of hope and inspiration in a world where being in the spotlight may frequently feel lonely. Her commitment to mentoring not only enhances her legacy but also makes sure that country music will always be at the forefront of cooperation and support. Lainey is contributing to the development of a bright future for the genre by fostering emerging talent and promoting diversity, one in which each artist is given a chance to shine and tell their own story to the world.

# CONCLUSION

## Reflections on Her Journey

Lainey Wilson's story of perseverance, sincerity, and empowerment through her path in the country music industry is captivating. From her modest upbringing in Baskin, Louisiana, to her ascent to prominence as a leading voice in the field, Lainey has continuously personified the essence of the genre, which is broad in its impact and reach but rooted in intimate narrative. Because it captures the feelings and experiences that are universal in real life, her music strikes a chord with listeners. It serves as a constant reminder that the fundamental purpose of country music is to share the truth about our lives.

In addition to changing Lainey's career, her distinct take on country music has opened doors for a new wave of musicians. She promotes diversity and teamwork, creating an atmosphere of camaraderie in the business that goes beyond rivalry. Lainey's dedication to coaching up-and-coming talent is a testament to her character; she knows that real success comes from encouraging others to pursue their own goals in addition to one's accomplishments. She supports the upcoming generation of performers by imparting her knowledge and experiences, allowing them to develop their own identities while paying tribute to the rich history of country music.

By fusing her artistic talent with her personal story, Lainey has produced a sound that is both modern and richly entrenched in history. Her willingness to try new genres while adhering to her narrative heritage is evidence of the diversity of her craft. Her music is approachable to a wide range of listeners due to her ability to close the gap between the past and the present, ensuring that the fundamentals of country music will never stop changing.

Lainey is a tribute to the strength of will and sincerity as she keeps shattering stereotypes and redefining what it means to be a country music singer. Her experience inspires us to accept our narratives, value our viewpoints, and stand by one another while we forge on. Lainey Wilson's voice is a unifying force in a society that frequently tries to divide people, encouraging us all to find common ground by sharing our experiences with love, heartbreak, and resilience.

The influence Lainey Wilson has had on country music goes far beyond her awards and chart achievements. She is the epitome of the genre, promoting inclusivity, honesty, and the narrative power of stories. We can anticipate that as her journey progresses, she will continue to serve as an inspiration to everyone who dares to dream, not only those in the music industry. Lainey's narrative serves as a helpful reminder that achieving success is rarely a straight line but rather a stunning tapestry made of tenacity, desire, and the guts to remain true to oneself. Lainey Wilson is set to make a lasting impact on the music industry with her singing, mentoring, and unbreakable spirit. She will make sure that country music's heartbeat endures for many years to come.

www.ingramcontent.com/pod-product-compliance
Lightning Source LLC
Chambersburg PA
CBHW050311230526
45471CB00005B/2124